COME NOW TO THE WINDOW

Poems by

Ann Iverson

LAUREL
POETRY
COLLECTIVE

ACKNOWLEDGMENTS

"A Formal Dinner" published on *www.achemagazine.com*. "The Cats" published in *Miller's Pond*. "Come Now to the Window" published in *A New Name for the Sun* (Laurel Poetry Collective, 2003). "A Nightmare after My Father's Stroke" and "Breast Cancer" published in *Water~Stone*. "The Intimacy" published on *www.drawingworkshop.com*. "Unholy Sonnet" published in *The Oklahoma Review*, electronic. The author's work has also appeared in *Margie: American Journal of Poetry*, and *Chronicle Alternative*.

Love to my family—Jack, Arline, Randy Sr., Randy Jr., Margie, Claudia, Mary, Jeannie, and all who follow. To the undying energy of the Laurel Poetry Collective and my poet companions, Kirsten, Marie, Carol, and Teresa. Thanks to my friends who believe in me as a poet. Admiration for Deborah Keenan and Jim Moore, whose generous contributions to poetry and dedication to my poems make this book possible.

Passage from #16 by Anna Akhmatova, translated by Jane Kenyon with Vera Sandomirsky Dunham from *Twenty Poems* (St. Paul, MN: Nineties Press and Ally Press, 1985). Passage from "Still Game" by Marie Luise Kaschnitz, translated by Lisel Mueller from *Selected Later Poems* (Princeton, NJ: Princeton University Press, 1980). Passage from "Directions to the Lady Lever, Port Sunlight" by Jude Nutter from *Pictures of the Afterlife* (Cliffs of Moher, Co. Clare, Ireland: Salmon Publishing Ltd., 2002). Passage from "Fill and Fall" by Li-Young Lee from *Book of My Nights* (Rochester, NY: BOA Editions, Ltd., 2001). "A Disorganized Man" modeled after "A Precise Woman" by Yehuda Amichai, translated by Benjamin and Barbara Harshav from *A Life of Poetry* (New York: Harper Perennial, 1994). The title of "Unholy Sonnet" is borrowed from Mark Jarman's "Unholy Sonnets," from *Questions for Ecclesiastes* (Ashland, OR: Story Line Press, 1997). Passage from a letter of Rainer Maria Rilke to Lou Andreas-Salomé, translated by Stephen Mitchell in his notes on the Seventh Duino Elegy in *The Selected Poetry of Rainer Maria Rilke* (New York: Vintage Books, 1989). "Pygmalion and Galatea" inspired by oil on canvas, *Pygmalion and Galatea*, Jean-Léon Gérôme, Metropolitan Museum of Art (Nineteenth Century European Paintings and Sculpture Galleries). "Blue Enters Me" inspired by oil *Isle of Shoals*, Childe Hassam, Minneapolis Institute of Arts. "The Intimacy" inspired by a pastel painting by artist Harold Stone from his *Intimacy Series*. The painting can be viewed at *www.drawingworkshop.com*.

"The Cats" was set to letterpress broadside by Regula Russelle, Laurel Poetry Collective.

ISBN 0-9728934-3-1
Library of Congress Catalog Card Number applied for.

Printed in the United States of America.

Published by LAUREL POETRY COLLECTIVE,
1168 Laurel Avenue, St. Paul, MN 55104
www.laurelpoetry.com

Book design by Sylvia Ruud. Bird graphic by Ann Iverson.

For Every Window:

parents, their beaming light

sisters, their reflection

husband, his vision

CONTENTS

I

How does it happen that you [poetry] come to moan under my small high window?

From #16 by Anna Akhmatova

MUSE

When the owls died,
I shot forth the hoot

first image in my mouth.
I came to it like a sinking village

between the continents of.
I mouthed blue rivers

never swimming near the rocks
found the deaf, dumb mute

of my own bones
then drank like a living reptile.

RAPUNZEL

Rapunzel never wanted
to leave her tower really,
not for anyone.

Only wanted the world
to come up to her
level of gravity,

like flying in a plane
away from everyone you love
on the day you need it most.

Her hair
has nothing to do with
her story.

A FORMAL DINNER

I am seated at both ends of the table

eating for two: the poet and the one who isn't.

I pass the silver platter

and say thank you.

The one who isn't watches

while the one who is

lifts the lid of language.

One of us loses her appetite.

One of us loses her manners.

Isn't frantically leaves the table.

Is sits alone in the dark.

PYGMALION AND GALATEA

Pygmalion and Galatea, oil on canvas, 1890
Jean-Léon Gérôme

She is half woman, half sculpture.
Victim of his passion.

Legs are stone. Waist is flesh.
She secures his seeking hand which is to touch.

Yet slides, I with her, into him young artisan,
who steps up once and into her.

His blood pours through her veins.
Her flesh turns ghostly, smoothly white.

Cupid of draw and release
      of fletching feather,

      of broad end set
      aims from the dark corner.

The arch of desire settles in her back.
Shoulder blades dimple to life.

Her buttocks is a half a moon
her spine a river to desire.

Though her face is hidden in the kiss,
she is the perfect woman.

The mask of tragedy on the shelf
can not close its mouth of terror.

BLUE ENTERS ME

Isle of Shoals, 1899 oil
Childe Hassam

Whose shores are shaped
like the many faces
of those who want to enter
the sea.
Of those who entered
the sea.
Their jagged expressions of pain,
a rudimentary belief that water
will save you.
The hemisphere tilts
and blue spills out of me
pours from me.
As though I was made
to contain the ocean
not the ocean containing me.

WATER

Witnessing my own body: rivers, creeks,
crevasses. For all of my life, I've refused my body.
Like a part of a street that has been cordoned off,
even before the crime is committed.

Symbols

The Catalpa will always be

a man of contradiction

leafing giants in my heart.

From his branches bird-son sings

excuses of departure.

It's a sad sort of ticking

for the mourning dove

who knows she can never appear

as anything but my plural desire

for the sad synonym of snow.

The sound of a truck driving away

becomes a pink dusk

on the last day in March.

In the mirror perennials gasp

at my new vision for them.

9:32 P.M.

My Shadow
slunk in its chair.
My hands small
moving mountains
that arch and crest
become anything I want,
if I perform.
Now an evil wolf.
Now a tarantula.
Now an ostrich.
Now a Brachiosaurus,
or any of my unknown
wide-mouth monsters.
Now a bird in flight
from itself.
Better than I
and lighter
my shadow is.
No cruel tongue.
No heart to carry resent.

WHAT THE TAXI DRIVER DOESN'T ASK, DOESN'T SAY

Where are you really going?
You seem young
in the moon's rearview mirror.
My take on life.
I'm sure you understand.
What is yours?
Oh, I see.
But you must need more than
that one small satchel.
Do you really want to leave
a warm house
with a light still burning before you?
It must have been the snowstorm
that led you to me.
Oh, how I have plummeted and dragged
to pick up the best of you.

EFFECTS OF A STALKER

Life is broken at the root;
your hair lay all around.

Gather one strand at a time;
it will take that long.

For months the body
has been his pastime.

The proof is in
a windshield note.

Plant new seeds.
Hope that some

come up as
you.

Or
eyes

in the back of your head
so you too

can always
be watching.

When Riding

Often when riding, you look out into the pastures
cattle sleeping, wildflowers taking over the air

and life is absent of fear. You see the eyes of
one lone doe searching for water and suddenly

you cannot call yourself back. The thrush of something
sends itself down your throat. You belong there.

The whippoorwill. The same one you heard out your
bedroom window, as a girl, is in the field you are standing in.

GOD TO MARY

I didn't have to look very far to find you.
In my heart, I knew it all along.

When I first heard the cries to save the world,

I found you in the field,
hushly singing to the lambs at close of day.

I didn't ask you then but walked down the road at set of sun,
heard the bells across the silver air, calling.

Don't think it just a notion;
I thought of only you for such a long time.

PASSAGE

I feel room inside for three of me
Outside for one
Inside for none of you
Outside for more.

Inside for seven mothers,
Outside for Time. I tell Time assertively:

Lie down now in my broken lawn chair
Under the great Catalpa.
If you turn the chair a few inches to your right,
You can see and smell both gardens.

It Doesn't Happen Very Often

that I cry myself to sleep
but when it does,
I let it go
I help it run
as though I were shoveling
the coal into the furnace
of a mighty ship,
as if it's
the one thing that I can do
to help
this world keep going.

II

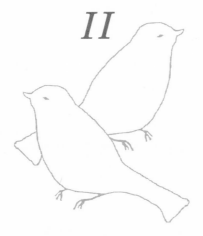

Still game for this:
To pull up
The window shades and discover…
Still game to go out
Down the old cobbled street
Passing windows.

From "Still Game,"
Marie Luise Kaschnitz

HUMMINGBIRDS

Now five have come to dine
off the steady banquet of pink geranium;
the only sound is the whir of their wings.
Soon it will be autumn.

One is a window washer on scaffolding;
it pauses as though to sigh
before cleaning the next section.

But something, as always,
will abruptly reel up the ropes of summer.

Winter House and Rising Words

One cat spreads over the table
the weight of his body on the answering machine.

Week-old messages rise while I panic
that some have been erased.

Not for long. Whoever needs or wants me
will find me. Even if it takes years.

The radiator emits energy like a preacher
who won't move from behind the pulpit.

The heat of words rises.

By now every poem and every sermon
is clinging to the dome.

ATTAINMENT

On cold days
when I let them out
they poke their heads
from the door,
stretch their forearms out,
wiggle their ends,
shake the hay
furiously
as if they had just
sat for hours
preparing their taxes.

They roughhouse
in the yard
as though the news was good:
tails in motions
that could knock over a small child,
flipping circles
above the crests of snow;
then rumbling
towards the house
halfway licking each other
growling and tearing
so all the way in love.

THE ENGLISH SETTER, ABSCOND

What will I say upon my return
    after my bowls are filled
        and the gates are closed
            the cats looking in at me
                like some worn-out prodigal?

How will I reply, when the questions are asked?
    Where have you been—why didn't you call?
        But I have seen the world
            golf courses, highways, bridges, and lakes.

I've been queen of the field,
ears flapping and brushing the breeze
with softball leagues
I've gleefully laughed and cruised the air,
touching every base

        but   slowly   I   came   down

as it began to storm, the shadows dissolving
into small, economy cars,
the wind a gust, umbrellas inside out.
Not a one knew my name.

I remembered my bowls,
the toy robot I had gnawed in the yard,
the flowering columbine I had meant to snap off
before this flight.

That chunk of stew meat
a pat on my head
one foot of the bed
one belly rub
the painting of an ancestor hunting.
My master's certain whistle and tone
of love and reprimand.

CAT AND DOG SLEEPING TOGETHER AT THE FOOT OF THE BED

As minor protagonists
they enter each other's dreams
the cat sighs
the dog purrs.

Some nights in sleep
in every house
or worn-out world
each thing is in agreement.

THE SICK CAT

I am already late for the rush of traffic
but instead I open the fridge
and spoon the
cottage cheese
slowly into a human bowl.

Stroke his long back once,
lock the door and leave for a life
where not a single small thing
needs me or cries out.

THE CATS

To find such glory in a dehydrated pea
on the tile between the stove and fridge.

To toss the needs of others aside
when you simply aren't in the mood for affection.

To find yourselves so irresistible.

And always in a small spot of sun,
you sprawl and spread out the pleasure of yourselves

never fretting, never wanting to go back
to erase your few decisions.

To find yourself so remarkable
all the day long.

At Odds

Then the air is still
even the animals take their places silently.
It is not serenity here
as when a house is tranquil at dusk
while one reads and the other writes

but a disabling hush.
The dogs notice it best when things are ill at ease.
Dinner is made, the dishes are left,
the walk stays filled with snow.

Animal Requiem

When the first snow falls I think of you.
How you died on the morning of Saint Valentine.

How you could say nothing of your pain
and if you could, you would have chosen silence.

I'm not sure where to place this animal sorrow.
Or if I could ever put it down for good.

Some things in life are more weightless than others.
For years, I've kept your collar and tag

inside an old coat pocket.
It seems like the only right thing I can do.

PECULIAR BUTTERFLY ON THE PURPLE CONEFLOWER

I was only looking for weeds to pull, half tired from the sun
when there she was plunging her proboscis

into the ovary of the three-foot coneflower.
She was much like a nurse taking a specimen.

As if she would whisk away to her laboratory.
As if she would tell me later the flower has two months to live.

THE WEEK YOU ARE AT KABEKONA BAY

I am home floating
through the house
as an apparition
watering plants
pondering verse
spooning cottage cheese
straight from the carton,
the fridge door wide open.

The cats barely speak;
the dogs collapse
at the edge of the bed.
I wash my face and
look in the mirror.
I can see through myself.

III

...from every window
you'll watch brightness drop in great panels
over the water. You might think these are doorways
sprung open in the world
and left unguarded, but this is something
only the dead know, and the dead
tell us almost nothing about where they belong.

From "Directions to the Lady Lever, Port Sunlight,"
by Jude Nutter

SYMPHONY

Since there is no one here
to argue this point:

I think my parents
loved each other

and their love was very much like
a long symphony,

in which I'll never understand
the meaning behind

the great and forceful gestures
and the restless abundance of song

and the cacophony and the sorrow.
And the accord which finally comes

to only those in old companionship.
Yes, to only those who've had their fill.

THE FOLLOWING

When my father died
he brought my mother back to life

and they rose together in spirit form
to give me strength to work.

They drove with me to school.
They sat with me and ate with me.

They taught for me
and thought for me.

They heard me say at home
They are all over me.

They shopped with me
and watched me more.

In a massive, lonely parking lot
of a mall that once had promise

I looked up to the cold night sky
and saw their shape and form.

PERHAPS WHAT THE DEAD DO

Perhaps what the dead do
is what they did on earth.

If that's the case, then the creases
in my mother's hands are still

stained brown from refinishing
furniture, this bed I sleep in.

Perhaps she is still stuffing tissue
into the right side of her bra.

And my father at the kitchen table of Heaven
is still wondering aloud.

Though this time I answer him.

BOAT ASHORE

For Claudia and Kenneth

Leaving my body was simple,
the boat did all the work.

This new river you'd like it.
The edges are speckled

with driftwood shaped into
small animal forms.

Free of undercurrents,
I worry about nothing.

I hear you say
that I was innately good

and now I finally fit into my goodness
like an old vest

which slips perfectly
around each shoulder.

But I remain to be
so curious about you.

There's a gentle cove up ahead
where I plan to take your mother

and talk with her
about what it is like

to still love you.

PACKING THE CLOTHES OF THE DEAD

I made room for a few of your belongings

next to mother's in the knotty pine chest on the porch

while the giddy March sun

talked behind my back. Whispered

I don't know what to do when she's like this

Call me crazy but after ten years

her dresses still carry her scent.

I held one paisley blouse to my face

a purple skirt to my waist

tucked my hair into the soft folds

of a mink hat.

Turned my face this way that way

while the sun and the snow and the grass and the breeze

gabbed on and on and on.

THE DAY BEFORE THANKSGIVING

You've been gone long enough now
so when you come back in dreams
the part of me which was frightened
is no longer and so this frightens me,
that the water is getting wider.

I think heaven has changed you so much
I can hardly recognize you anymore
when you knock on the door of slumber
donning yet another fresh face.

Or that living has made me so tired
I don't have the energy
to wonder what my life would be
had you stayed.

I don't agree with those who say the dead don't care.
I don't believe they are so far removed from having a body
that they forget about the weight we carry.

When the dream snaps, you are just as lonely.
For why else would you have come,
if it wasn't because you longed for me?

UNTITLED

I can't imagine having the weight of an infant on my breast
or breasts so swollen in anticipation for those feedings.
I can't imagine a tiny, gummy sucking
then a simple *coo coo*
or the nest a newborn makes of the woman's body.
I can't imagine my breasts or being solely responsible
for providing another's only nutrition.
And, these days, I can't imagine, any more, so many things.

What I can imagine is the look in her eyes
after they had removed one of hers.
As they wheeled her to recovery
how my father slowly and awkwardly
bent to kiss her unscarred cheek.

MOTHER'S DAY

But I never did

place the flowers around the stone.
I made an attempt with one
silk rose
a white silk rose,
stopped for my father at the home
but he was already in hospital gown
ready for bed at seven thirty.
So I just went home to a silent house,
quiet as the flower
after the nectar has been taken.

You see, she just keeps falling deeper
like a stone thrown to the lake.
She fades and fades
and nothing can stop the sinking.

But deep inside, when I least expect her,
she rises in me like a beautiful letter never sent.

Seven Years after Her Death

In her cubicle
after grading the last few papers,
a small silence,
in which
she honestly thinks
she can give her mother
a quick call
since no one
is using the phone,
the office empty
of everything
but the perfunctory
gesture of love.

A Nightmare after My Father's Stroke

The Devil drives a black Model T
over the old neighborhood.
His face is quite similar to a
National Inquirer tabloid:
a chalky, smoky image
pouring out of a volcano
or some other natural disaster.
He flies swiftly in his car
with many passengers
who appear to be waving
like beauty queens
or else for help.
It is a catastrophe;
I am separated from those I love.
I am digging through rubble.
The transition is instant:
I am in the Devil's backyard.
He is grilling steaks for his guests.
I know no one there.

FOR THE FIRST THREE MONTHS

For the first three months of my father's stay
at the nursing home, he wept a lot.

The first two weeks he cursed us,
struck at my sister.

I felt like I was pregnant
and the only fitting name would be pain.

NURSING HOME

Inside Frank Sinatra is singing
How do you lose yourself to someone but never lose your way?

I know the answer. But it just doesn't work.
Instead I clean my father's glasses, scrape

old food from his shoes, wash his bad ear.
And since he has no choice but to stay

I tell him of myself.

Now, Speaking for My Father

Every word of his I've wanted and waited for
seems a distant overtone

of an a cappella choir singing sacred hymns
that rise up in me while I am driving in my car.

They pour out above the music on the radio
and I sing in fervor

as though robed again in cobalt blue and golden collar,
with movement and connection to the lyric

and the force and close harmony of second soprano
gripping hands with the first,

an entire body of voices joining hands.
I am there and it happens.

When it's done, I just keep driving.

IV

*As long as night is one country
on both sides of my window, I remain a face
dreaming a face
and trace the heart's steep path.*

From "Fill and Fall" by Li-Young Lee

WATCHING THE 1996 OLYMPICS WITH MY FATHER

The strongest man in the world
could have lifted my Datsun
in the October blizzard of '91.
Where was he then?

Now he's genuflecting
touching his forehead, chest,
left shoulder, right
with his first two fingers.

He is so strong and kind
as he weeps for the crowd,
genuine as he attributes
body mass to his father passed away.

The man in the wheelchair, barely able
to aim the spoon, shakes his head in awe
the clarity of such strength
or maybe disbelief.

Some potatoes enter
some fall.

POLITICAL AGENDA: SIDEWALKS AROUND ALL NURSING HOMES

When we go to visit, we'd rather stroll him
through neighborhoods
with people loving each other,
or not, it doesn't matter. Observe:

In summer, of course, pedigreed dogs could growl mutiny
behind fences,
or just scruffy ones, who patrol the blocks
with an odd sense of government then expect to lick our hands.

Perhaps, a cat or two and a toddler on training wheels,
or just a woman in a halter top,
shouting through an open window
with what we feel to be exuberance.

In autumn, we might as well stumble across one of those
colossal caterpillars, inching humbly up a trunk,
prepared to build its temple
and change its life completely.

And in winter, no ice, but manger scenes,
houses shining like the second coming
while we try to guess electric bills,
then stop to pull his hat snug over his ears.

In spring all is exposed in its true nature:
the old rusted station wagon with the leaking head gasket,
the milestone of our walks. Heaps of leaves someone never bagged.
The smells of lovely earth and the busy chattiness of clean-up.

In summer again, because the sidewalks could easily take us
through the years of his silence,
the dandelions might tell us if he liked butter or not
while we held one under his chin.

BIRD SANCTUARY

The bird is a creature that has a very special feeling of trust in the
external world....That is why she sings in it as if she were singing
within her own depths; that is why we so easily receive a birdcall
into our own depths;...indeed, it can for a moment turn the whole
world into inner space, because we feel that the bird does not
distinguish between her heart and the world's.

Rainer Maria Rilke

Though the birds behind this glass are voiceless,
they once had lives filled with responsibility.
Toting hay, breaking earth, singing to us
from their own depths of love.
Here their food is proportioned in plastic containers
attached to the corners of their world.
Seed, seed, no real meat,
not much to work for.

~

My father isn't interested, at all, in the birds.
He likes it better when I speak for him,
telling the new social worker that he was a milkman
for thirty some years
lugged it through rapid water and snow,
grew the finest of eggplants,
which would put any purple to shame.
Had a wife and five daughters and a house just a mile away.

But actually, he's even more interested in death
and how it will be. Though I don't know this for sure
and don't even like to think it; but the way he looks over
the top of his glasses at me as though to say *just a while longer*
as he would, if I lost patience watering his tomatoes.

~

Behind the glass, they must be singing;
I like to think of it this way anyway,
the end: the indigo streaks of feathers on a bird's wing.
Or one in a cap to say a life was good.
The indecipherable song of the elderly
and how to some thing, somewhere
it all must make sense.

I want to think Rilke had it wrong.
Really, isn't it the bird who receives our final call?
And she knows, without a doubt,
because of this, that her heart
is very, extraordinarily different from the world's.

Breast Cancer

One time while painting in an unventilated space
my husband said, "Ann, breasts absorb everything,
every toxic fume and chemical there is."

~

I began to think of all the breasts in the world:
upright and alert in uncomfortable under-wire bras
or maybe weary and hanging with no support at all
vulnerable and innocent breasts.
Albino, cream chocolate, mint, bruised, bitten,
tangled, tired, silicone, yellow,
happy east and west.

~

Canine mammary cancer spreads identically
as it does in a woman:
Lump, lymph nodes, lung, back, brain.
The very obedient dog began to wet the carpet
about a year after the malignancy was removed.
That night after supper her legs gave out
and the cat came to touch noses.
The collar and tags are what they gave me.
My mom just loved that dog.

~

I have four sisters, which makes this fear tenfold.

~

For goodness sake, Mother,
you settle in my heart like a house at night.
The slowest creaking memory sinking deep into the earth:
I am four, you bathe.
I peek through the keyhole.
I hear singing from the tub,
your brassiere hanging from the doorknob.

HANDEL NEEDS ME

Those rare moments
when I can see directly through
feel him on the other side.

Like someone watching
a lover bathe
behind a translucent blind.

THE INTIMACY

The Intimacy Series, 1998 pastel by Harold Stone

The pink continents of his chest.
The blue river of her back.

Let those be your landmarks.
May those be the places that you know.

See how through the years
your face becomes the same

as that which you love.
If you love the trees

your kiss will
leave a green smudge.

If you love a crooked shadow
follow it anyway.

When you can't look me in the eyes,
feel my heart pounding against yours.

A DISORGANIZED MAN

after Amichai's "A Precise Woman"

A man turns the days to shelves
where I might store love
if I can't use it all today.
A man with a body set loose
stalks around in underwear.
A man with a breakable heart
never finds order to his grief;
even his passionate love cries
pile up on each other
like mail on a desk:
wild wolf, serious wolf
then eagle, deer, eagle.

MORNING GLORY VINE

One year
as late as October
it crawled its tangled
journey
up the cyclone fence
the trellis archway
the apple tree
was eye
to eye
with us
in our second-story bedroom.
We talked about it often,
our own flag of red apple and blue glory.
For how could we have
ignored the beauty
which followed us
that year
we married in July?

SONG OF SOLOMON

Drawing you as though
your body has the answer
needing to say it,
to dwell there.

Finding you daily
among the daily
in every room we enter
and become.

Answering you
as one answers the sky
with words that have wings
and a reason.

Collecting you,
dispersing you
as day
releases night.

Measuring you
as yards of fine fabric
to see how much of your skin
I can draw from its luscious bolt.

SUMMER

I've made hanging planters out of my mother's
antique ceiling light fixtures,
though I've risked to have them swing
beneath the apple branches
rather than over the French provincial sofa
as she did years ago.

Up north, I've used up every little gadget I found
when cleaning out my parents' attic.
The old camp knife
which folds out into eleven utensils,
I hung above the sink with the ivory-handled spatula
and the old popcorn griddle.
The small glass base from a 1920s water fountain
I turned upside down for birdseed,
though no birds have partaken.

I think I was good to my mother while she lived
and I visited my father often.
Right here, this summer
what else would I have myself say?

AND SO IT GOES

I want to think that you were comfortable
with dying, but I never thought to ask.
For to you, it seemed a kindly neighbor
merely coming for a cup of flour,
and you were less intimidated by her
than of the real women on our block.
Why did you always suffer
from what the neighbors thought?
If they thought anything
about our dandelions and Creeping Charlie,
always more tenacious
than the rose, which withers
at just the thought of pain.
When the man next door went to his garage
to put a bullet through his head
was it then you began to pass along to me
that life is indeterminable?
Was it then that you showed me?
What is it then, that you showed me?
You were blessed to die the perfect death
of simply never waking.
Your heart finally leaning its spade against the fence.
I want to think that's how it went,
but, perhaps, your eyes were open
to see the colors of her winter coat
plodding up the walk.
How politely death can borrow. How discourteous life can be.
Did he shut his eyes before he pulled the trigger?
I want to think that you were happy while *you* lived
but, then again, I never thought to ask.

Unholy Sonnet

Title after Mark Jarman

Two Easters ago I went to stay at my father's vacant house,
then up for sale. I closed the door and locked it,
while the thought of Christ
rising from the dead hovered over like a bird.
I felt holy in an unholy way.
If I can believe in the power of fourteen lines,

I can believe in anything. I can believe that our holiness
is gesture. The hand that reaches to dry our tears.
That the decisions of love are impossible. If you leave someone
for good, Christ will watch you. If you stay with someone forever,
Christ will watch you. He will never comment. He will never
give you a sign, not even a finger pointing that your leaving is wrong,
or a palm up for stop, or arms flagging us to come on home,
or a shrug to say that he simply does not know.

EXACTLY

Is how you died.
To the point.
With no abstraction.

But the three and a half
approximate days
of labored breath

and dripping morphine.
Each breath you took
was a colon:

Saying more
is on its way.
We fed you water

on a sponge stick
and your little tongue
lapped it up.

Though your halfway eyes
were inexact and your
spirit neither here nor there.

EATING IN SUMMER

Time passes into the mouth of summer.
I eat everything in sight: the cardinal,
the dianthuses, the fallen apple branches.

The mind reserves a place for the beauty
you cannot digest. Don't worry,
you'll choke up bad dreams.

They'll never go down. They'll never
kill you. The other night
with my mouth wide open to the dark

I dreamt that my mother, dead now
twelve years, didn't love me anymore.
I clenched my jaws and locked them,

so no more bad could enter.
I'm careful now to peel away
the hard skin of everything

I eat on summer nights.
Even if it's rare and beautiful
and brightly dressed.

DISTANCE

For many months after your death
I chose music to be the unfamiliar space you entered

and I sanctified your new territory alone in my car
with the song playing loud and the windows rolled up tight

so that you could not escape the small, modern temple
I had built for you.

Assuming you would never want to leave,
I thought of only myself

and of what other ways I could keep you trapped
within my song-filled chamber.

Patient you were to wait with me so long.

When the time was up you knew what must be done.
You freed my hand to walk.

The farther you got, the larger you became.
The further you get, the smaller I become.

COME NOW TO THE WINDOW

If you were a window, I could perch on the sill of my pain,
sigh, *aah, here is the sky.*

But history is a walking bird
lusting for the hover, the flutter of

without ever loving a view.
Yet the flush of this night. Must take it in:

the distant dog's moan; the young cat's song; the steady
arrhythmic breathing of that which has never worked.

Damp cloths on a silent forehead,
a lesser, whispered story for you of me: a child articulating

this art for a mother's sore, diabetic eyes,
a particle of stilled love bringing

fingers to your fevered face, a *coo coo*
from the skimming bird brought back into season.

Come Now to the Window is ANN IVERSON's first collection of poetry. She is a graduate of both the M.F.A. and M.A.L.S. programs at Hamline University. A poet who enjoys experimenting in the visual arts, she is interested in the visceral connection between the poetic and visual image. A sampling of her artwork can be viewed at *threecandles.org/featured.html* under the link to Deborah Keenan's collected work. An educator for twenty-two years, Ann has taught at The Loft and currently teaches humanities and writing at Dunwoody College of Technology. She is presently working on her second book, yet to be titled, and on editing a small collection of Rumi translated by Leo Parvis.

L A U R E L
P O E T R Y
COLLECTIVE

A gathering of twenty-three poets and graphic artists living in the Twin Cities area, the Laurel Poetry Collective is a self-funded collaboration dedicated to publishing beautiful and affordable books, chapbooks, and broadsides. Started in 2002, its four-year charter is to publish and celebrate, one by one, a book or chapbook by each of its twenty-one poet members. The Laurel members are: Lisa Ann Berg, Teresa Boyer, Annie Breitenbucher, Margot Fortunato Galt, Georgia A. Greeley, Ann Iverson, Mary L. Junge, Deborah Keenan, Joyce Kennedy, Ilze Kļaviņa Mueller, Yvette Nelson, Eileen O'Toole, Kathy Alma Peterson, Regula Russelle, Sylvia Ruud, Tom Ruud, Su Smallen, Susanna Styve, Suzanne Swanson, Nancy M. Walden, Lois Welshons, Pam Wynn, Nolan Zavoral.

For current information about the series—including broadsides, subscriptions, and single copy purchase—visit:

www.laurelpoetry.com

or write:

Laurel Poetry Collective
1168 Laurel Avenue
St. Paul, MN 55104